Norbert Kürlis

The Secret of Past Lives

Norbert Kürlis

The Secret of Past Lives

Echo of Souls

Imprint

© 2025 Norbert Kürlis

Publisher: BoD · Books on Demand GmbH, In de Tarpen 42, 22848 Norderstedt, bod@bod.de
Printing: Libri Plureos GmbH, Friedensallee 273, 22763 Hamburg
ISBN: 978-3-7693-5188-0

Content

Foreword

Over the years, I have often found that conversations with friends, acquaintances, and companions naturally turn to a fascinating and enigmatic topic: what happens to us after death. It is a question that has intrigued humanity for centuries, regardless of age, background, or belief system.

These discussions have left a deep impression on me. Everyone has their own ideas, hopes, and sometimes fears. While some firmly believe in reincarnation or life after death, others see death as the final conclusion. But what if there is more? What if our souls embark on a journey, if our existence does not end with our physical demise?

Exploring these thoughts has inspired me to write stories. Stories that are not only products of imagination and speculation but are also shaped by the dreams, beliefs, and experiences of the people around me.

With this book, I invite you to embark on a journey – a journey into the world of soul migration. Each story is a standalone adventure dedicated to the unknown. They are meant to provoke thought, inspire dreams, or perhaps simply entertain you.

I hope that as you read, you not only find joy but also discover new perspectives. Perhaps you may even recognize your own thoughts or questions that have long occupied your mind.

In this spirit: Let us take a glimpse behind the veil together.

Warm regards,
Norbert

Introduction

Have you ever wondered what happens when our life comes to an end? Where does the soul go when the body stops breathing? Some say it flies to the heavens, while others believe it returns to Earth to begin something new.

In these stories, you will experience the most exciting, humorous, and mysterious journeys that souls can undertake during their wanderings. Sometimes, they arrive in places filled with wonders. Sometimes, they encounter other souls with something important to say. And sometimes, they must make difficult decisions to discover who they truly are.

Perhaps you'll realize that within you, too, lies a soul full of adventure – ready to explore life's greatest mysteries.

Are you ready for the journey?

The Melody of the Past

The piano music fell silent, and a gentle murmur rippled through the opulent hall of the Grand Hotel "Eternal." Alexander, the new bar pianist, let his hands rest on the ivory keys for a moment before gently closing them. He had been playing all night, melodies that seemed to have forgotten time, carried along by the atmosphere of the centuries-old hotel.

"A break," he murmured to himself, rising and letting his gaze wander across the high ceiling and gilded chandeliers that must have witnessed so much – wars, lavish parties, lost loves.

At the bar, the bartender greeted him with a warm smile. "Mineral water, as usual?"

"Yes, thank you." Alexander leaned against the counter and accepted the glass. As the bartender stepped aside, Alexander glanced into the bar mirror.

But instead of his own tired face, he suddenly saw something that took his breath away.

A young woman, beautiful, with dark curls and a shimmering dress reminiscent of a bygone era, stared back at him. Her face was sorrowful, but her eyes seemed to smile, almost as if she recognized him. Alexander jerked back, the glass clinking on the counter. He turned quickly, but no one was behind him.

"Is everything alright?" the bartender asked, stepping closer with concern.

Alexander pointed with a trembling hand at the mirror. "There... there was someone. A woman. She... she was standing right behind me, but now she's gone."

A faint smile crossed the bartender's face, mixed with a touch of resignation. "Ah, it's happened again."

"What do you mean?" Alexander stared at him, confusion evident in his eyes.

The bartender leaned on the counter, his tone quieter, almost confidential. "Every new pianist sees her eventually. She belongs to this place, to this bar. I've never seen her myself, but the stories – I know them all. Some say she was the pianist here before the First World War changed everything. Her name was supposedly Claire."

"Claire..." Alexander whispered the name as if to taste it. "But why? Why does she appear?"

The bartender shrugged. "Maybe she just can't leave. Maybe it's the music that keeps her here. They say she was brilliant – the best pianist of her time. She supposedly died young, of a broken heart. And since then... well, she seems bound to this place."

Alexander was silent. He stared into his glass, then back at the mirror. The woman was gone, but he felt her presence lingering.

"And now? Should I keep playing?" he finally asked.

The bartender nodded. "You should. Maybe she's listening. Maybe that's all she needs – someone to keep playing."

With a slight shiver, Alexander returned to the piano. As he struck the first notes, the melody sounded warmer, fuller, almost as if an invisible hand were guiding him. And deep within, he knew: Claire was still there, a quiet melody within the old walls of the Grand Hotel.

Encounter with an Old Soul

When Anna stepped into the old café, she felt a strange tug in her chest, as if an invisible thread were guiding her to a long-forgotten place. The café was cozy, almost unremarkable, with wobbly wooden tables and faded photographs on the walls. Yet something about the atmosphere felt familiar, like a dream she couldn't quite grasp.

Anna ordered a tea and let her gaze wander. In one corner sat an old man engrossed in a book. His silver hair fell messily across his face, yet he exuded a peculiar sense of calm. When his eyes suddenly lifted and met hers, time seemed to stand still for a moment.

"Why don't you join me?" he said, his voice deep and gentle. Anna, surprised by his directness, hesitated only briefly before sitting down with him.

"I don't know you, and yet..." he began, leaving the sentence unfinished.

"I feel like I've met you before," Anna replied, before she even knew why she said it. It was absurd, and yet it felt right.

The man smiled, his eyes sparkling as if he were about to share a story only he knew. "There are encounters that transcend time. Some souls are connected, no matter how many times they are reborn."

A shiver ran down Anna's spine. She had never delved into such topics, but something about his words struck a deep chord within her.

"Why do I feel like you know me?" she asked.

"Perhaps because I do," he replied softly. "Not in this life, but in a previous one. I was... a teacher to you, you might say. You were full of curiosity and light, though your path was not easy."

His words brought flashes of memories that didn't seem to be hers: a room full of books, the crackling of a fire, a voice teaching her to practice patience. It was as if a hidden window within her had been thrown open, allowing her to glimpse something beyond her understanding.

"And now?" she asked, her voice barely more than a whisper.

"Now I meet you to remind you of something. You are here to complete what you began. But only you can know what that is."

The encounter lasted perhaps an hour, perhaps two. When Anna left the café, she felt changed. The old man had given her nothing concrete, yet his gaze, his presence, seemed to have opened a door within her.

From that day on, she began to notice the subtle signs in her life: an old passion for writing that she picked up again, an inexplicable calm in difficult moments, and a newfound trust in the flow of things.

The old man disappeared, as if he had never existed. Yet Anna knew he had touched a part of her soul, an echo from another time, reminding her of who she was and where she was going. The encounter with the old soul was not an ending but a beginning.

The Familiar Garden

Karen had no idea why she decided to drive to the small town on the edge of the hills that afternoon. It had been a spontaneous decision, triggered by an image in a travel brochure: an old garden with a weathered stone bench, surrounded by lush green scenery. The place had something about it that irresistibly drew her in, as if it were calling her.

When she arrived, the town embraced her with a strange mix of novelty and familiarity. The narrow cobblestone streets, the half-timbered houses with their weathered wooden facades, the scent of lavender in the air—it was as though she had experienced it all before.

Karen followed the signs to the garden, hidden behind a small stone wall. When she pushed open the heavy iron gate and stepped inside, a wave of emotion washed over her. Before her stretched an oasis of wild greenery. Roses climbed trellises, and tall, ancient trees cast protective shadows over the moss-covered ground. In the center of the garden stood the stone bench from the brochure, yet it didn't feel foreign.

She walked toward it slowly, her fingers brushing the leaves of the bushes as if testing whether the place was real. A faint tingling sensation ran over her skin. When she reached the bench and sat down, she felt a deep pull in her chest, so strong it momentarily took her breath away.

"I've been here before," she whispered. But it wasn't just a guess. It was certainty.

Karen closed her eyes, and images began to surface in her mind. A woman in a white dress, sitting on the same bench with a book in her hands. A man whispering something to her as he stood beside her. Laughter echoing between the trees. A promise, whispered like a secret: "I will always be here when you need me."

The images were so vivid that for a moment, she thought she was dreaming. But when she opened her eyes again, the garden was the same. The man and the woman were gone, but the feeling of their presence lingered.

Suddenly, she heard footsteps behind her. She turned and saw an older gentleman wearing a straw hat, looking at her with curious eyes.

"Strange to see you here," he said. "I've never seen you before, and yet... you remind me of someone."

Karen smiled uncertainly. "I feel like I know this place. It's as if I've been here before."

The man nodded slowly. "Many people say that when they come here. But with you... I don't know. Maybe you really have been here, a long time ago."

They spent the afternoon talking. The man told stories about the garden, about the people who had lived there, and about a couple who had come together in that very spot decades ago. A woman in a white dress, a man with a gentle voice.

When Karen left the garden later, she felt light and fulfilled, as if she had regained something she thought she had lost long ago. She didn't know if the memories she had experienced truly came from a past life, but that didn't matter. The garden was a part of her, and she was a part of it.

For many years afterward, Karen returned to the garden again and again, each time feeling as though she were coming home. It was a place that existed beyond time, a space where the present mingled with the infinite. And perhaps, she sometimes thought, she had never really left at all.

The Familiar Town

Andreas wasn't entirely sure why he had chosen this town. He had simply boarded the train without much thought. It was a spur-of-the-moment decision, born out of a strange restlessness that had accompanied him for weeks. As the train pulled into the small station, his eyes fell on the name of the place: Ravensholm. The name stirred an inexplicable echo within him, as if calling forth something familiar that he couldn't quite identify.

The town looked like something out of an old fairy tale. Narrow alleys wound their way between dark, timber-framed houses, their windows shuttered with heavy wooden panels. A light rain fell, and the wet stone streets glistened dimly in the gray afternoon light. Yet despite the unfamiliarity, Andreas felt oddly at home.

As he walked along the main street, he couldn't shake the feeling that every corner, every detail, was somehow known to him. The old clock above the café, the statue of a man holding a book in the marketplace, the fountain with its stone lion's head—all of it evoked memories that couldn't possibly be his.

He turned into a side alley without knowing why and found himself standing before a small shop, its window cluttered with antiques. He hesitated briefly before stepping inside. A bell above the door rang brightly, and an old man with snow-white hair looked up from a dusty book.

"Can I help you?" the man asked, his voice carrying a curious warmth, as though he were greeting an old friend.

"I'm not sure," Andreas replied honestly. "I just... somehow ended up here."

The man smiled and gestured to a chair. "Sit down. No one ends up in Ravensholm by accident. This town has its own ways of drawing people in."

Andreas sat down and began to share his strange feeling—that everything here felt so familiar, even though he was certain he had never been there before. The old man listened attentively, not interrupting once.

When Andreas finished, the man laid the book he had been holding on the table in front of him. It was an old journal, its cover made of worn leather.

"Read it," the man said softly.

Andreas opened the book and began to read. The handwriting was old but clear, and the words told the story of a man who had once lived in Ravensholm. The more Andreas read, the stronger the feeling grew that these stories were his own. The places described, the thoughts, even the decisions—they all felt strangely aligned with him.

"This… this is me," Andreas whispered eventually.

The old man nodded slowly. "Sometimes souls return to places that meant something to them. Perhaps to understand. Perhaps to finish something."

Andreas didn't know how to respond. He stared at the book in his hands, as if it could offer him answers.

"What am I supposed to do now?" he finally asked.

"Follow the traces," the man said. "The town will show you what you need to know."

Andreas left the shop with the book tucked under his arm. The alleys seemed even more familiar now, as though they were guiding him. And as he walked, he began not only to remember the town but also to remember himself—a life he had once lived here.

The Lantern at the End of the Alley

The city lay shrouded in mist, softening everything into shades of gray. The streetlights cast flickering pools of light onto the pavement, and somewhere in the distance, the echo of footsteps resounded. Emilia pulled her coat tighter around herself and quickened her pace. It was late, and she was on her way home from an exhibition that had captivated her much longer than she'd planned.

When she turned into a narrow, almost forgotten alley, she suddenly stopped. The silence here was different, heavier. At the end of the alley stood an old lantern, its light strangely warm, almost inviting. Directly beneath it sat a woman on a low bench, cloaked in a wide, dark shawl.

"An unusual place for a rest," Emilia said cautiously, unsure why she felt compelled to speak.

The woman lifted her head. Her face was etched with deep lines, and her eyes were so bright they seemed to glow in the lantern's light. "Sometimes it's not the place that's unusual but the time," she replied, her voice floating like a whisper in the air.

Emilia stood rooted to the spot. There was something... different about this woman. "Are you waiting for someone?" she asked.

The woman smiled, and her gaze held a knowledge that Emilia couldn't grasp. "I am always waiting. But today, you've come."

"Me?" Emilia frowned. "We don't know each other."

The woman shook her head. "Not yet. But I know your heart, child. It carries a burden you've brought here tonight."

A shiver ran down Emilia's spine. How could this stranger know such a thing? And yet, her words struck her like an arrow.

"I don't know what you mean," Emilia said, even though she did.

"You seek answers," the woman continued, ignoring Emilia's protest. "You wonder why the world feels so heavy. Why some leave, and others remain. Why everything you do isn't enough to ease the pain."

Emilia swallowed hard. The memory of her father, who had passed away a year ago, rose unbidden. The unspoken words, the guilt she felt for not being there when he left.

"Who are you?" she finally asked.

The woman stood slowly, her cloak swirling around her like smoke. "I am no one and everyone. A voice from yesterday, a shadow in today. Call me what you will. But tonight, I am here for you."

"Why?" Emilia's voice was barely a whisper.

"Because you need someone to tell you it's okay to let go."

Emilia felt tears streaming down her cheeks. The woman's words seemed to come from a depth she couldn't understand but instinctively knew was true.

"I should have been there for him," Emilia said at last, her voice breaking.

The woman stepped closer, her hand cold yet comforting as it rested on Emilia's shoulder. "He knew you loved him. That's all he needed to know. You carry a guilt that isn't yours to bear. Leave it here, with me."

Emilia took a deep breath, and suddenly, the mist seemed lighter, more transparent.

"Will I see you again?" she asked.

The woman smiled. "Perhaps. But if not, you now know where to go when the weight becomes too much."

Then she stepped back, and as Emilia blinked, the woman was gone. The lantern had gone out, leaving the alley quiet and empty.

Yet in Emilia's heart, a spark of light remained, guiding her through the night—and perhaps, just maybe, beyond.

The Whispering Stone

Clara couldn't quite explain why she felt compelled to visit this ancient monastery in Avignon. Perhaps it was the image she had seen in a travel guide: the massive vaulted ceilings, the intricate stone carvings that seemed to tell stories. Or maybe it was the mention of a hidden manuscript said to have been concealed there in the 14th century. Yet, as she crossed the threshold, it was as if a familiar melody began to play softly within her—a tune she couldn't place but couldn't ignore.

The air inside was cool, tinged with the scent of aged stone and faded incense. Afternoon sunlight filtered through the high windows, casting luminous patterns on the floor. Clara paused, her fingers brushing against the rough walls. Suddenly, a wave of emotion washed over her—longing, fear, a strange blend of loss and familiarity. It was as if the room itself breathed, holding the memories of those who had once been there.

Her steps carried her deeper into the hall, where a towering stone pillar rose before her. As she lifted her gaze, she noticed a small symbol etched into the stone: a circle bisected by a single line. She couldn't explain why, but she recognized it. It was as though she had drawn it herself, perhaps in another time.

Without warning, she closed her eyes, and images began to form in her mind. She saw a young woman dressed in a heavy gown of burgundy velvet standing in that very spot. In her hands, the woman held a book bound in dark leather. Beside her stood a man, his face obscured by a deep hood. He spoke softly, his voice carrying an urgency she couldn't decipher. Though the words were unintelligible, Clara felt their meaning: they spoke of something forbidden, something that had to be preserved at all costs.

The scene shifted. She watched as the woman hid the book in a small niche beneath the engraved pillar. Her hands trembled as she moved the stone to conceal the hiding place. The man placed a hand on her shoulder, whispering something that sounded like a vow.

Clara's eyes flew open, and she gasped for air. The hall was silent, yet the images had etched themselves into her soul. She reached out to touch the spot on the pillar where the woman had hidden the book. Was it still there? Or had it all been a figment of her imagination?

"Are you all right, madame?" a voice asked from behind her. Clara spun around, startled, to see an older man with kind eyes. He wore the uniform of a museum guide and held a stack of brochures in his hands.

"Yes, I... I just thought..." She trailed off, unsure how to explain what she had just experienced.

The man nodded as if he understood. "Many people feel something within these walls. They hold the stories of those who lived here."

Clara wanted to respond, but the words caught in her throat. Instead, she asked, "Do you know anything about an old book that was said to be hidden here?"

The man regarded her for a moment before speaking slowly. "There's a legend about it. A book of knowledge, hidden during times of persecution. But no one has ever found it."

Clara only nodded, yet deep within, she knew the book was real. It was waiting. And perhaps, she thought, it was waiting for her.

Reunion in Mönchengladbach

Lena loved exploring unfamiliar cities, and this weekend she had chosen Mönchengladbach. The narrow alleys of the old town, the small cafés, and above all, the imposing abbey church had drawn her in. But as soon as she arrived, she felt an unexplainable tension in the air—a sense of anticipation that mirrored her own inner restlessness.

She stood in front of St. Vitus Church, the heart of the city, gazing at the tall Gothic windows that cast shimmering colors inside. It felt as though the walls were calling her. Without hesitation, she stepped inside.

Inside, she was enveloped by deep silence, broken only by the faint murmur of a few tourists wandering through the nave. Lena stopped and took a deep breath. The scent of incense, aged wood, and stone was strangely familiar. She didn't know why, but she felt she knew this place, as if something important had happened to her here.

As she walked slowly through the church, her eyes fell on a side alcove where a small candle flickered. A man stood there, and she caught sight of him only from the corner of her eye. Something about him stirred a strange unease in her. His posture, the way he gazed at the light—it was as though she had seen him before. She paused and tried to recall, but the images in her mind were blurred.

Suddenly, he turned around. Their eyes met, and for a moment, time seemed to stand still. Lena's heart raced. The man was about her age, with dark brown hair and striking features. But it was his eyes that captivated her—deep and filled with a melancholic wisdom she couldn't explain. It felt as though he recognized her just as much as she did him.

He approached her slowly. "Excuse me," he said in a warm, calm voice, "I know this might sound strange, but... do we know each other?"

Lena stared at him, unable to speak. Her thoughts raced. Why was he asking the very question that was burning inside her?

"I... I'm not sure," she finally replied, her voice quiet and uncertain. "But it feels that way."

A small smile played on his lips, and he nodded. "Maybe we should talk for a moment. Sometimes coincidences aren't just coincidences."

She agreed, and together they left the church. They found a small café nearby, where the afternoon sun streamed through the windows. His name was Markus, and the longer they talked, the more they felt that their meeting wasn't by chance.

As they shared stories, strange memories began to surface. Markus spoke of dreams he often had—of a woman in a long dress working in an old library. Lena suddenly remembered visions of a man faced with a difficult decision while a burning city loomed in the background.

"This sounds crazy, but I think we've known each other before," he said eventually. "Not in this life, but in another."

Lena nodded slowly. It didn't make sense, and yet it felt so right.

The afternoon passed, and as dusk fell, they returned to the church together. There, in the quiet of the ancient building, they found no clear answers, but an unspoken connection that deeply moved them both.

Perhaps, Lena thought, they had begun something long ago that had been interrupted. And now, in this life, they had the chance to finish it.

The Soul Reunion in Merano

It was a mild night in Merano, and the old parish church of St. Nicholas stood serene and majestic under the vast starry sky. Its tall walls and tower, silhouetted against the darkness, seemed to bear witness to something ancient—and on this night, they would do so once more.

Three figures moved silently through the narrow streets, without footsteps, without shadows. They were like wisps of mist, translucent yet distinct enough to be perceived—if anyone had been able to see them. They were no longer human but souls, free from the confines of the world. Once, their names had mattered: Anton, Elias, and Maria.

Many years ago, still bound to their mortal shells, they had made a pact. They had been young, full of ideals and secrets, and during a trip to Merano, they had whimsically—or perhaps instinctively—decided that their souls would reunite here when their lives had come to an end.

And now, the time had come.

Anton was the first to arrive. His form shimmered faintly, surrounded by a delicate flicker as if he were made of light. He hovered before the church, his soul still restless, as if unable to fully shed the burdens of his life.

"Elias? Maria?" His voice was not a voice but a thought spilling into the air. The response came quickly.

Elias appeared, emerging from the darkness. His form was slightly more defined, the edges of his figure sharp, as though he had retained more of himself. "Anton," he said—or thought. "You're here. I knew you'd be the first to arrive. Always so punctual, aren't you?"

Anton might have smiled, had souls been capable of such gestures. "And you're still the one who always finds humor in everything. Where's Maria?"

No sooner had he spoken than she appeared. Maria was a breath of elegance, her presence surrounded by an almost imperceptible warmth. She glided gently toward them, the air around her seeming to whisper.

"You were waiting for me," she said, her words tinged with a quiet melancholy. "It's been so long, and yet it feels as if it were only yesterday."

The three souls stood—or rather hovered—in a circle before the church. Their thoughts —words, emotions, memories—began to intertwine. They didn't just see each other; they felt the essence of one another.

Anton remembered the afternoons in the little café in their hometown, the long conversations about life and death. Elias saw an image of a warm summer night, the night they had vowed their bond would never end, not even in death. Maria felt the old familiarity—a mix of love, friendship, and something that had never quite been spoken aloud.

"And now what?" Anton finally asked. "We're here. But for what? Was it just a promise? Or is something waiting for us?"

Elias laughed—a strange, silent laugh that felt more like a gust of wind. "Maybe we just wanted to see if we'd keep our word. There are no maps for the journey we're about to take."

Maria gazed up at the church. "Perhaps we're meant to move on. But then again, maybe not. What if this is enough? To remember, to be together?"

The stillness of the night enveloped them, and for a while, no one spoke. Then they began to drift into the church together. Their forms grew fainter, their shapes nearly merging with the shadows. They carried no answers, but they carried one another, and that seemed to be enough.

The church walls embraced them, their whispers echoing softly among the ancient stones. Whether they would remain there forever or move on, no one could say. But the church in Merano had kept its promise: it had brought together three souls that had never truly been apart.

In the Dream, Eva meets her Mother

Eva had always had a special connection to her mother, even after her death. But nothing could have prepared her for the dream that visited her on a chilly November night. It wasn't like a normal dream; it was vivid, clear, almost tangible.

She saw her mother as she remembered her: in a flowing dress, with warm eyes and a gentle smile. She stood in a bright room, its walls pulsing with light.

"Eva," her mother said, her voice both loving and urgent. "You must go to the church. There you will understand."

Eva wanted to ask which church she meant, but before she could find the words, the image faded. She woke up with a strange feeling in her chest, a mix of unease and anticipation.

The next morning, she couldn't shake the dream. Her mother's words echoed in her mind: "You must go to the church." But which church? She lived in Rostock, a city full of historical churches. It could be any of them. After some hesitation, she decided on St. Mary's Church, an imposing Gothic building in the heart of the city. Perhaps, she thought, something would become clear there.

As she entered the church, a sense of awe washed over her. The high vaulted ceilings, the dim light, the quiet shadows – it was as if the space itself was breathing. Eva walked slowly through the nave, her footsteps echoing softly on the stone floor.

Her gaze fell on the Astronomical Clock, a masterpiece from the 15th century. She stopped in front of it, not knowing why. The clock didn't just show the time; it also tracked the movements of the planets and the liturgical calendar. Her eyes were drawn to an inscription she had never noticed before: "The truth will reveal itself in the light." Suddenly, it was as if something clicked inside her. Her mother's words, the dream – everything made sense. She remembered an old family secret, something her mother had once told her: A precious letter from her great-grandmother had been hidden in one of Rostock's churches to protect it from destruction during the war. St. Mary's Church had to be the place.

With her heart racing, she approached the priest, who was lighting candles at the altar. She told him about her dream and what she was searching for. The priest, initially skeptical, finally led her to an old chest that had been in the church's archive for decades.

Together, they opened the chest. Inside, among yellowed documents, lay an envelope marked: "For those who come." Eva took the envelope with trembling hands and opened it. The letter contained a message from her ancestor, speaking of love, hope, and the importance of keeping the family's story alive. It was a legacy meant to be passed down through generations.

Tears ran down her face as she read. Now she understood why her mother had appeared to her in the dream. It had not been just a message; it had been a mission to preserve something valuable and pass it on.

As she left the church, her heart felt lighter. The dream had not only led her to an old truth, but also to a new understanding of her own roots.

Memory of Terlan

Heinz was not a man who indulged easily in nostalgia. His life had been shaped by pragmatism, by clear lines and firm decisions. But for some time now, he had been experiencing a strange feeling, a tightness in his chest that grew stronger each day. It had started with dreams – vivid, almost tangible images of orchards, of the sun reflecting in ripe apples, and the scent of fresh earth.

In one of these dreams, he saw himself standing under the trees with a large basket full of apples. He wore simple clothes, unfamiliar yet strangely comforting. Beside him stood a woman whose face he could barely make out. She was laughing, and the sound of her voice was like a melody he had forgotten.

The next morning, the feeling was still there. He couldn't help but wonder what it all meant. Heinz had never worked in an orchard, let alone lived as a fruit farmer. His life had always unfolded in offices, conference rooms, and busy cities. But these images – these memories – felt more real than much of what he had experienced in his current life.

After weeks of increasingly intense dreams, he decided to investigate. An internet search led him to a place called Terlan, a small village in South Tyrol known for its fruit orchards. The pictures he found of the area made his heart race. Something about it seemed so familiar, as though he had walked through these landscapes himself, as if it were calling to him.

One sunny autumn day, Heinz packed his suitcase and drove to Terlan. As soon as he reached the village, he felt a strange sense of familiarity. The gentle hills, the rows of apple trees, the little houses with their red roofs – it was as though he had come home. He walked through the narrow streets, his steps guided by an invisible force, until he stood before an old farm. The sight of the weathered wooden gate triggered a flood of emotions in him. "I've been here before," he murmured, though his mind told him that was impossible.

An old man came out of the house and looked at him curiously. "Can I help you?" he asked with a broad South Tyrolean accent. Heinz paused for a moment, then decided to be honest.

"I'm not exactly sure why I'm here," he began. "But I have the feeling I know this place. It sounds crazy, but... I think I was here once, in a past life."

The old man furrowed his brow, but there was an expression of interest in his eyes.

"That's not the craziest thing I've ever heard," he finally said. "Come, let me show you something."

He led Heinz through the gate into the courtyard. The surroundings were just like one of his dreams: the large barn, the rows of fruit trees, the sun filtering through the leaves. The old man told him that the farm had once belonged to a man named Johannes, who had passed away many years ago.

"Johannes was a fruit farmer, a very good one. But he also had a tendency to be thoughtful, just like you," the old man said with a smile. "They say he spent his best years here. Maybe that's why you feel this connection."

Heinz stayed in Terlan for a while. He helped

the old man on the farm, picked apples, dug in the earth, and felt a deep peace spread through him. Whether Johannes had truly been a past life of his, he would never know for sure. But during those days, surrounded by the fruit trees and the silence of Terlan, he found something he had long been searching for: a sense of home.

Return of the Past

Lennart was not religious, but he had sought silence – the silence of nature and meditation, to escape the relentless noise of the world. For years, he had lived in seclusion in a small house on the edge of the forest, far from the city he had never liked. Here, he found comfort in the daily rituals of Zen, in listening to the wind as it passed through the trees, and in the shimmering images his thoughts painted.

But one morning, while walking through the forest, he encountered her for the first time: a young woman sitting at the edge of the woods, writing in an old notebook. Her eyes were like those of a person who knew more than they could put into words. And yet, Lennart had the feeling he already knew her.

"Good morning," he said cautiously.

"Good morning," she replied with a smile that touched Lennart deeply. It was a smile he had seen before, on a face he thought he had long forgotten.

She introduced herself as Marlene and

explained that she had moved into the house next door. Her voice was calm, almost melancholic, as if she were in a conversation with time, a conversation that had long since begun.

In the following days, they met again and again at the edge of the forest, where they sat together in silence, often without words. It was a connection that went beyond the obvious. Lennart felt that he was finding a depth in her that seemed not of this world. Her laughter reminded him of his grandfather, who had passed away in the 60s. One evening, as they sat side by side and the golden rays of the sun illuminated the forest floor, Lennart asked her, "Have you ever felt like you were someone else before?"

Marlene looked at him thoughtfully for a moment, then nodded slightly. "Yes, sometimes I feel like I have lived another life. I dreamed of a farm, an old house, and a man who often worked in a garden. He had gray hair and a calm, strong presence. It feels like I was there, like I was that man."

Lennart's heart suddenly began to race. The description of the old man, the farmer – it was exactly the man he had known as a child:

his grandfather. A wave of recognition washed over him.

"What exactly did you dream?" he asked, his voice tinged with disbelief.

"It was simple things," she said. "The smell of freshly mown grass, the sound of chickens in the yard, and the feeling of earth under my fingers. But then... then came death. It crept in suddenly, and I knew it was time to go. But in another moment, I felt like a child in a mother's arms – everything was peaceful, everything was clear."

Lennart felt as though the ground beneath him might give way. It was as though his grandfather's spirit had found him again through this young woman. It was more than just a feeling of familiarity – it was a realization that this soul was now living again in a new form.

"Marlene," he whispered finally, "do you believe it's possible for a soul to return? That it lives on in another body?"

Marlene looked at him with a slightly confused expression, but her answer came without hesitation: "I don't know, but I feel it. I feel like I have something to finish – something I didn't do in this life."

In the following weeks, Lennart began to dive deeper into his meditations. He sought answers within himself and found peace in the idea that death was not the end, but merely a transition.

Marlene and he had long conversations, during which she often spoke of the dreams that had haunted her in recent years – of a life that intertwined with Lennart's own memories.

It was a slow, healing process, which eventually made Lennart realize: His grandfather's death was not the end, but the beginning of a new chapter. And perhaps it was the start of something he had never expected: the return of a loved one in a different form.

One evening, as the autumn wind blew through the forest and the stars sparkled above them, Lennart took Marlene's hand and whispered, "There is no farewell. Only new paths."

Past Steps

It was a rainy afternoon when I wandered through the streets of this city for the first time. I had no plan, no particular reason to be here – just the desire to go somewhere where no one knew me. The air smelled of wet asphalt, and the rain beaded on the shiny cobblestones that stretched like an old mosaic through the narrow alleys.

But the further I walked, the stranger I felt. The streets, the shops, the old lanterns that seemed to belong to another time – all of it awakened an inexplicable sense of familiarity. It was as if I had known this city before, even though I was sure I had never been here.

Then I stopped abruptly. In front of me was a small café with a faded wooden sign above the door: Café Aurore. The clinking of dishes and muffled voices came from inside as a guest opened the door. My heart beat faster. This café – I knew exactly what it looked like inside, even before I had taken a single step inside.

I hesitated but eventually walked in. The

room was warm, smelling of freshly baked bread and coffee. An old wall clock ticked softly, and on the back wall hung a painting of a river winding through a golden landscape. I knew that painting would be there.

"Can I help you?" asked the waitress, a kind woman with a gentle smile.

"No, I... I just wanted to look," I stammered, but I knew that wasn't the truth. Something pulled me to a particular table in the corner, beneath the clock. I sat down there without thinking. My hands rested on the table, smooth and cool. I could imagine sitting here – but not as myself.

Suddenly, a memory surged into my consciousness. I saw myself in this café, but I was not me. I was a man with graying temples and a worn, heavy coat. My hands were larger, rougher, and I held a newspaper whose date didn't match my current life. It was the year 1938.

I rubbed my temples, confused by the intensity of the image. But the more I thought about it, the clearer everything became. I remembered my name – Henri. I had been a simple bookbinder, often sitting here to think, write, and watch the people passing by.

The life of this man, my former self, unfolded in my mind like the pages of an old book. I remembered the war that came and changed everything. The lost love that had kept me tethered to this table, where I waited for a return that never happened.

A tremor ran through me as I realized I hadn't come here by chance. This city, this café – it was a part of me. And even though decades had passed, an echo of my old self still lived within the walls of this place.

I sat in the corner for a long time, my gaze fixed on the clock, which slowly ticked on. The past and the present were intertwined, like two rivers merging into one stream.

When I left the café, I no longer felt like a stranger. I was a traveler between two lives, a bearer of memories that had not been lost but had slept deep within my soul until I was ready to find them again.

Echo of Love

Anna and Elias had met in a way that was neither spectacular nor unusual. It was a rainy afternoon in a small bookstore when both reached for a tattered copy of Rilke's poems at the same time. Their hands touched, they smiled at each other, and a conversation began, which ended with a shared coffee. But from the very beginning, there was something strange between them – a familiarity that went beyond what strangers should feel for each other. It was as though they already knew each other's words before they were spoken. And as their relationship grew, they felt more and more that their connection was extraordinary.

One evening, while they sat together on the couch talking about their childhoods, something strange happened. Anna told Elias about a recurring dream that had followed her since her youth: "It's like a scene from an old film. I see myself in a long, blue dress at a ball. It's somewhere in the 19th century. A man dances with me, and I feel incredibly happy. But then... then he has to leave. It's as if he disappears forever."

Elias, who had been listening attentively until then, froze. "I had a dream like that too," he said softly. "But from a different perspective. I'm an officer in uniform, and I dance with a woman in a blue dress. She's beautiful. But then I'm called – a war begins. I say goodbye to her, and she cries. It feels so real every time."

A shiver ran down both their spines. It was as if their dreams were pieces of a shared past. From that moment on, they began to discover more and more similarities. Their interests, their quirks, even some details from their childhood seemed to overlap. Anna loved a particular waltz that Elias strangely knew how to play on the piano, though he couldn't remember ever having learned it. Both of them felt a deep melancholy when they looked at old 19th-century paintings, as if these images were awakening memories they couldn't place.

Their curiosity finally led them to a therapist who specialized in past life regression. Hesitantly, they agreed to undergo hypnosis together. The sessions revealed astonishing things: they both saw themselves as a couple in the 19th century, separated by a war that had destroyed their lives. Anna died young of a broken heart, while Elias fell as a soldier, never to return.

But their love had apparently survived death. Their souls had found each other again, in another time, in another life.

"Was all of this a coincidence?" Anna asked one evening, as they lay together in bed. "Or were we meant to find each other again?"

Elias took her hand and held it tightly. "I don't believe in coincidences, Anna. It feels as though the universe brought us together again to finish something we couldn't complete back then."

From then on, they viewed their relationship with a new depth. Every conversation, every laugh, every touch was a step that brought them closer to something bigger than themselves. And the longer they were together, the more it seemed as if they could read each other's thoughts.

"I was just about to say that I love you," Elias began one evening, as they sat by candlelight. Anna smiled. "I know. I was just about to say it too."

Perhaps it was a coincidence. Perhaps it was destiny. But for Anna and Elias, it no longer mattered. They knew that their love was timeless, a bond that endured through space and time.

Anne and the Old Soul

It was a cool spring day when Anne went to
her mother's grave. The trees were in full
bloom, and the scent of fresh grass mingled
with the damp earth. The cemetery was quiet,
the birds chirping, and only the rustling of
leaves in the gentle breeze broke the silence.
Anne was alone. She had never really
processed the years since her mother's death,
but today, she felt the urge to finally find
peace. Slowly, she knelt beside the grave,
removing the withered flowers and placing
fresh ones. The words she whispered were
always the same, a mixture of sorrow and
gratitude.

But today, something was different.

A cool breeze brushed her neck, and she
heard the soft crunch of footsteps behind
her. She turned around and saw an old
woman walking toward her with slow,
deliberate steps. Her face was lined with deep
wrinkles, but her eyes, shining in an intense
blue, held a strange warmth, as if they knew
something Anne had never understood.

"Excuse me," Anne said, rising in confusion. "I thought I was alone here."

The woman simply nodded and smiled gently. "I didn't mean to intrude," she said in a calm, almost melodic voice. "But I can see the pain in your eyes. Your mother, she was a strong soul."

Anne stared at the woman, a strange sense of familiarity washing over her. She didn't know why, but it seemed as though she had seen these eyes before. Perhaps in a dream?

"How do you know that?" Anne asked hesitantly. "My mother has been dead for a long time."

The old woman slowly sat on a nearby bench and motioned for Anne to sit beside her. "I'm not here to frighten you," she continued. "Sometimes, in this world, you encounter the souls of people who have long passed. They are not really gone; they live on in us."

Anne swallowed. "What do you mean?"

"I knew your mother, but not in the way you might think," the woman said with a slight smile. "I'm old, yes, but the years have not only told me many stories. They have also given me the ability to see what remains hidden to others. You and your mother...

you've shared many lives together. She was your teacher, your friend, and also your sister in other times."

Anne blinked, and a cold sensation crept up her spine. She wanted to say something, but the words stuck in her throat.

"You might wonder why you don't remember," the old woman continued. "Why you don't recall all the other lives you shared with her. Sometimes, the memory of the soul is a mystery. But one thing is certain: you carry many parts of her within you, and you will always find your way to her, no matter how many lives may come."

A strange calm began to rise within Anne, a connection to something beyond words.

"What do I need to do to find her?" she finally asked. "How can I retrieve the lost memories?"

The old woman stood up and placed her hand on Anne's shoulder. "There is no simple answer, my dear. But you will know when the time is right. Sometimes, you just have to listen and feel what the soul is telling you."

With those words, the woman turned and slowly walked along the path leading into the shadows of the trees. Anne wanted to call out, but when she turned around, the woman had simply vanished.

She was left alone at her mother's grave, but the sense of emptiness had disappeared. Instead, she felt embraced by a memory she didn't yet fully understand but that she deeply sensed within herself. Perhaps what she was seeking wasn't to be found in the past.

Perhaps it was in the connection she still had with her mother – through all time.

Slowly, she placed her hands on her chest, closed her eyes, and listened to the quiet whispers of her soul.

Anne and Andreas

As Anne spoke the last word, she sat beside Andreas on the sofa, her hands clasped in her lap as if trying to hold on to her own thoughts. The words she had just shared with him weighed heavily in her mind. They held something mystical, something that didn't quite fit into the world. And yet, she knew they were true.

"And this just happens, with the grave care? An old woman telling me about my mother, about lives I've never lived?" Andreas looked at her with a mix of concern and interest. "Anne, you know you can tell me anything, but... this sounds like more than just a strange coincidence."

Anne nodded, her gaze far away as if she were still on the cemetery. "It felt so real, Andreas. This woman, she knew details about my mother, about us. And she spoke of past lives I can't remember. She said we had spent many lives together."

Andreas put the book he had been reading aside. "I can imagine," he said thoughtfully. "It reminds me of something that happened to me a few years ago. I never told you about it because I thought you'd think it was nonsense."

Anne turned to him, surprised. "What do you mean?"

"It was while I was fishing," Andreas began. "You know how much I love it, those quiet moments by the sea. I was alone on the pier when I suddenly felt like I wasn't alone. At first, I thought it was just a bird getting too close, but then I heard voices. Not loud voices, more like whispers, as if someone was standing right behind me."

Anne furrowed her brows. "And then?"

"I turned around and saw an old woman. She was dressed entirely in black, like I imagined women from old tales. Her eyes, Anne, those eyes... they had so much to tell. She wasn't looking at me, but staring out at the Baltic Sea, as if she saw something I couldn't see."

"And what did she say?" Anne asked, now fully immersed in the conversation.

"She spoke of past times. Of the years when

the Baltic Sea was still young, when people along its coast lived different lives. She told me about my grandfather, his youth, his travels—things only he could have known. She even said that I had met him in another life when we lived in another country."

Anne was silent, staring at him. "And what did you do?"

"I don't know," Andreas sighed. "It was all so strange. I wanted to ask her how she knew all of that, but before I could open my mouth, she just vanished, as if the wind had carried her away. I wasn't sure if it was all real or if I had just imagined it. But in that moment, it felt so clear, as if she had truly been there."

Anne reached for his hand and held it tightly. "Maybe it's those souls that connect us, Andreas. Those invisible threads that bring us together at the most unexpected moments in our lives. Maybe that woman just wanted to show us something today, to remind us that we are more than just what we see in this life."

Andreas looked at her, and for a moment, silence fell between them. Then he slowly nodded, as if understanding what she meant. "Maybe you're right, Anne. Maybe the truth is bigger than we can ever imagine."

Anne smiled faintly. "Maybe we're not as alone as we think."

"Maybe not," Andreas said, squeezing her hand. "Maybe we're all just searching for what we've lost."

And so they sat there, hand in hand, the words of the old woman and the memory of a strange encounter neither of them could forget, in their hearts. Time seemed to stand still as they gazed at life and the mysteries that lay beyond what the eye could see.

The Soul of Grandpa August

It was a quiet evening when Norbert entered the old family house, which had stood empty for years. The walls seemed to have absorbed time, the scent of long-forgotten memories lingering in the air. Norbert had often wondered if there was something special about this place, something that transcended the material world. Tonight, on this evening, he would find an answer.

He had spent the entire week thinking about why he was drawn here. The reason lay deep within him—he wanted to speak with his beloved Grandpa August, a man who had passed away in 1965. August had always been a source of wisdom for him, and even though he knew his grandpa had long since passed from this world, he felt a strong connection to him. Perhaps it was time for him to receive his grandfather's final piece of advice.

Norbert sat in the old armchair in the living room, which still smelled of tobacco and pipe smoke, even though Grandpa hadn't sat in it for decades. The chair was just as he remembered it—worn but comfortable. Lost in thought, he closed his eyes and remembered the many hours he had spent as a boy on his grandpa's lap, the stories of old times, and the wise yet simple way he explained the world.

Then there was a sudden, almost imperceptible crackling in the air, a chill breeze that swept through the room. Norbert opened his eyes and froze.

Before him stood a figure he instantly recognized. It was his Grandpa August. But he was not older; instead, he was young, in the prime of his life—the very man Norbert remembered from his childhood. He wore his beloved wool coat, and the expression in his eyes was the same as always: warm, inviting, and full of love.

"Grandpa?" Norbert could hardly believe his eyes. His voice was a whisper, yet the words fell like heavy lead in the room.

"You found me, my boy," the figure said, in the familiar, soothing voice of his grandpa.

"I've been waiting for you to be ready to talk to me."

Norbert felt as if his heart was beating faster. "How... how is this possible? You're..."

"Dead?" August gently interrupted. "Yes, that's true. But you must know that death is not the end, Norbert. There is so much more you can understand, if you allow it."

Norbert felt a knot in his stomach loosen. It was as though he was finally being freed from all the doubts that had plagued him in recent years. "I've missed you, Grandpa. So much. And I've wondered what happened to you, where you are now."

August sat down in the old chair opposite Norbert, and for a moment, it was as if time itself stood still. "I'm still with you, Norbert. I'm not really gone. The soul moves on, but it stays connected. You feel me because you're ready to listen to us, those who have already left."

"And what should I do?" Norbert asked, his voice now firmer as he understood the depth of the words. "How do I find peace?"

"You've always looked to the future, to your work, to your life. But don't forget that life also lives in the memories you keep. I'm a part of you, just as you are a part of me. Learn to understand this connection. The love we had for each other doesn't fade. It remains, through all time."

August reached for Norbert's hand, and for a moment, everything inside him felt calm and right. "Listen to your heart, my boy. It will always guide you. You just need to learn to listen."

"I always thought you'd give me one last piece of advice, Grandpa," Norbert whispered, lowering his head. "But I never knew how much you're still with me."

"I always will be," August replied with a smile, one that reminded Norbert of all the warm embraces he had received as a child. "Never forget, you're never really alone. You carry me inside you."

As Norbert felt his grandpa's hand in his, the figure began to slowly fade, as if blown away by the wind. Yet, his grandpa's words lingered, and in that moment, Norbert knew that he was never truly apart from him.

He opened his eyes; the room was empty again, but in his heart, he felt the connection to his Grandpa August stronger than ever. And he knew that he would never stop talking to him—in his memories, in his dreams, and in every decision he made in his life.

It was not the end. It was merely the beginning of a new connection that transcended time and space.

Anne in the Kindergarten

Anne had a restless night. She kept waking up, until finally, she drifted into a strangely clear dream. She was sitting on a wooden bench with her deceased grandmother, surrounded by a radiant garden. The air smelled of freshly mown grass and blooming flowers, but there was something else that captivated her completely: the voice of her grandmother.

"The soul, my dear," she said with a warm smile, "is like a bird flying between worlds. Sometimes it lingers in a garden like this, sometimes it moves on. But you mustn't be afraid. We all find our place."

Anne wanted to say something, but her voice stuck in her throat. Instead, she watched as her grandmother gently placed her hand on hers. "Don't forget, the connection remains. It will guide you, if you allow it."

Suddenly, Anne awoke. The morning sunlight streamed through the half-open blinds, but she could still recall her grandmother's words clearly. Her heart felt heavy and light at the same time, as if she had glimpsed a world she couldn't fully grasp.

The morning at the kindergarten started as usual. The children ran around laughing, painting colorful pictures or building tall towers with blocks. Anne tried to stay present in the moment, but the dream of her grandmother buzzed like a whispering wind in her thoughts.

As the children sat at their drawing tables after breakfast, little Lena approached her. She was holding a crumpled sheet of paper with a large, colorful heart drawn on it.

"Anne, can I tell you something?" Lena asked in a soft, yet insistent voice.

Anne knelt down to her. "Of course, Lena. What is it?"

The little girl looked around briefly, as if making sure no one was listening. Then she whispered, "I dreamed of a garden last night. It was really bright, and there was an old woman. She said the soul is like a bird that flies."

Anne felt her heart skip a beat. Her fingers unconsciously closed around the edge of the table. "What did the woman look like?" she asked hesitantly.

"She had a colorful scarf on and such a warm smile. She said everything would be okay."

Anne's throat tightened. That was exactly the description of her grandmother. Even the scarf fit—it was a family heirloom her grandmother had always worn. As Lena ran back to the other children, Anne stood frozen. Could it be that this dream was more than just a memory? Was it possible that her grandmother had spoken not only to her, but also to Lena?

Over the next few days, Anne became more attuned to the little signs of everyday life. She noticed that Lena was suddenly interested in topics she had never noticed before. Lena asked about stars, the lives of butterflies, and about death—questions that Anne sometimes found hard to answer.

One afternoon, when Anne took the children into the garden, Lena sat beside her with a handmade paper airplane. "Anne, do you think the bird will let me fly too?" she asked suddenly.

Anne looked at the little girl, who seemed so serious, as if carrying a wisdom beyond her years. "I think we all fly eventually," she answered softly. "But until then, we have plenty of time to explore the world."

Lena nodded. "Maybe the bird will meet your grandma again. She was nice."

Anne had to swallow, but a smile tugged at her lips. She had no answers to the riddles that life sometimes presented. But she knew that this encounter with Lena was no coincidence. Something had reminded her that the connection between worlds endures —through dreams, through words, and through the unwavering power of love.

That night, Anne slept peacefully. And in her dreams, the garden appeared again, the light, and the soft whisper of a bird soaring through the air. Maybe, she thought, her grandmother was still there, between worlds, offering her guidance.

Lena

Lena, now 25 years old, stood before the Colosseum in Rome. It was a warm spring evening, and the ancient stones glowed in the golden light of the setting sun. She felt deeply moved by the history of this place and sensed the vastness of time becoming tangible here.As she crossed the square, she noticed an older man sitting at the edge, dressed in ragged clothes. In front of him lay a small cup, with some coins clinking inside. Lena stopped and rummaged a euro coin from her pocket. She dropped the coin into the cup, and the man looked up. His eyes seemed unusually clear, almost penetrating."Grazie," he said softly. Then he added, "Sometimes we give something small and receive something great in return."

Lena smiled politely and was about to continue when the man suddenly said, "Your sister misses you."

She turned around, startled. "My sister?" she whispered. Her younger sister had passed away just a few months ago, a loss Lena had not yet processed.

"Yes," the man said, looking at her with a calmness that almost frightened her. "She wanted you to know: She's fine. She's like a bird flying free, just as you always wanted her to be."

Lena felt tears welling in her eyes. "How do you know that?" she asked, but the man didn't respond. Instead, he just smiled, as though he knew of secrets beyond understanding. When Lena blinked, he was gone. Only the cup remained, empty and still, like the evening around her.

Lena stood there for a long time before finally walking on, her heart heavy yet full of comfort. She knew she would never truly lose her sister. Some connections, she thought, are stronger than death.

A Near-Death Experience

Markus lay on the cold operating table. The harsh light of the lamp above him blinded him, and the sterile air of the room filled his lungs. The voices of the doctors and the monotonous beeping of the machines gradually blurred into a dull hum, until everything went silent.

Suddenly, there was a light. It was warm and inviting, radiating such intensity that Markus felt drawn to it as if by instinct. He didn't notice how his body stayed behind. Before him stretched a tunnel of light, and with each step, he felt peace and safety envelop him.

When he reached the end of the tunnel, the surroundings opened up into a wide, radiant meadow. The grass was lush and green, the flowers shimmered in colors he had never seen before, and the air was clear and pure. It was as if every worry, every pain, every fear had fallen away from him.

Then he saw them: figures that felt immediately familiar. His parents stood there, smiling, arms outstretched in an inviting gesture. His father, whom he had lost thirty years ago, looked just as Markus remembered him: strong, loving, and full of joy. His mother, whose gentle embrace had always comforted him, appeared as vibrant as she had before the illness had marked her.

Next to them, he recognized more faces. His grandparents, uncles, aunts, even a school friend who had passed away far too young. They all radiated a calm and love that deeply moved Markus.

"Markus," said his father in a voice so familiar and soothing that Markus felt tears well up. "You are not ready yet. But we are always with you."

Markus wanted to speak, wanted to stay, but he felt an invisible force slowly pulling him back. The meadow began to fade, the faces became blurry silhouettes, and the light gradually gave way to darkness. He wanted to resist, wanted to hold his father's hand, but it was too late.

With a sudden jolt, Markus opened his eyes. The harsh light of the operating lamp blinded him again, and the voices of the doctors became clear and frantic. "We got him back," he heard one of the voices say. His heart was beating again, heavy and tired, but he was alive.

A few hours later, Markus lay in his hospital bed. His wife, Anna, sat by his side, her eyes red from tears. She had firmly grasped his hand, as if to prevent him from slipping away again.

"You were almost gone," she whispered. "The doctors said it was close."

Markus slowly turned his head towards her. "Anna," he began with a weak voice, "I need to tell you something."

He told her about the light, the tunnel, and the meadow. About his parents who had welcomed him, and the deep peace he had felt. Anna listened, speechless, her eyes wide open.

"It was so real, Anna," Markus said at the end. "I don't know how to describe it, but I believe that death is not the end. It's a transition to something beautiful. And my parents... they're there. They're waiting for me, when the time comes."

Anna was silent for a moment before she squeezed his hand even tighter. "As long as you're here, Markus, that's all that matters," she said softly. But in her eyes, a mixture of astonishment and comfort reflected, which seemed to calm her heart.

Markus closed his eyes, exhausted but at peace. The memory of the meadow and the faces of his ancestors didn't fade. It was a truth he carried within him, a secret he would hold for the rest of his life.

The Voice of the Summit

The sun hung low over the mountains, and the light draped the rugged rocks in a golden veil. Jonas tightened his boots and slung his backpack over his shoulders. He was alone, following an old path that seemed nearly forgotten. The local who had described the way to him had only said, "When you reach the summit, you will understand."

Understand, Jonas thought. Understand why he was here? Why this vague longing had driven him into the mountains, away from the city, the noise, and the ever-same faces?

After hours of climbing, he reached a small plateau. The wind was biting cold, yet it carried a strange warmth, like a comforting hand on his shoulder. At the edge of the plateau, right before a rock ledge, an old woman sat on a flat stone. Her hair was snow-white, and she wore a simple dress that looked as if it had endured centuries.

"I'm glad you made it," she said without looking up. Her voice was quiet, but it echoed off the rocks, as if nature itself were repeating her words.

Jonas stopped, confused and a little out of breath. "How did you know I was coming?" he asked cautiously.

The woman lifted her head, and her eyes were as clear as mountain lakes—deep, unfathomable, and full of stories. "I sense those who seek. You are not the first to come here. But everyone seeks something different."

Jonas stepped closer and took off his hat. "Who are you?"

She smiled. "You're asking the wrong person. The question is: Who are you? And why are you here?"

He had no answer. Was it fleeing his old life? The sorrow for things he had lost? Or was it something he could not name?

"I don't know," he confessed finally.

"Good," said the woman, motioning toward the rock ledge. "Then you're ready to listen."

"Listen?" Jonas stepped carefully closer. Below him, the world fell into the abyss, a chasm of shadows and light. The silence was overwhelming, yet he thought he could hear something—a humming, like an ancient melody that seemed to be sung by the mountains themselves.

"The mountains remember everything," the woman said behind him. "The people who crossed them, the dreams that were born here, and those that ended here. Some souls linger because they cannot let go. Others stay because they guard what was. What do you hear?"

Jonas listened. The melody was stronger now, piercing him like a warm breeze. But then there were words. A whisper, soft and urgent: "You must let go."

"Let go?" Jonas repeated aloud.

"Only you know what you're holding on to," said the woman, and when he turned around, she was gone.

The stone where she had sat was empty, but there was a small object on it: a necklace with a pendant made of smooth green stone. Jonas carefully picked it up. It felt warm, almost alive.

With the necklace in his hand, he sat at the edge of the abyss. The melody of the mountains was still there, and with every breath, he felt the weight on his shoulders lighten.

As the sun disappeared behind the peaks, Jonas knew he was no longer the same. The mountains had taken something from him— or perhaps had given him something back. And he was ready to move on.

The Secret of the Grandmother

Peter sat alone in his small city apartment, the window slightly open to let in the mild summer night. The full moon cast silver light on the houseplants and the old family portrait on the wall. It was one of the few things he had inherited from his mother: a black-and-white photo of his grandmother, young, with a gentle radiance and a smile that seemed to say, "I know something you don't know."

He had always found the picture fascinating, even though he had never met her. His grandmother, Helene, had died long before he was born. But tonight, the picture seemed more alive than usual.

Peter ran his fingers over the frame. "What kind of life did you lead?" he murmured to himself, more to himself than to anyone else.

"A full life," answered a calm, warm voice behind him.

Peter froze. Slowly, he turned around, and his heart skipped a beat. There she stood, his grandmother Helene, exactly as she appeared in the photo, but now in flesh and blood. Her eyes sparkled, and her smile was as mysterious as it was familiar.

"Who... who are you?" Peter stammered.

"I am Helene, Peter. Your grandmother," she said gently. "And I am here because it's time for you to learn something."

His mind struggled to grasp what stood before him, but a part of him knew it was true. "How is this possible? You're... you're dead."

Helene nodded. "I am. But sometimes there are things that can't be said while we are alive. And some knowledge waits for the right moment to be shared."

"A secret?" Peter asked, still unsure if he was dreaming or awake.

"Yes," she said. "A secret that concerns our family, and one I must entrust to you."

She stepped closer, sat down on the old couch, and motioned for him to sit. Peter obeyed, his eyes fixed on her face, which was so familiar yet so foreign.

"Peter, in our family, there is a tradition that has been passed down through generations. We have all inherited something—a gift, if you will. It is not obvious, and it often reveals itself only when the right moment comes. But you carry it within you, just as I did and my mother before me."

Peter furrowed his brow. "A gift? What kind of gift?"

Helene smiled. "The ability to see the truth in people. Their deepest thoughts, their secrets. It is not a curse, but a gift, when you learn to use it properly."

Peter shook his head. "I... I can't do something like that."

"Not yet," said Helene. "But you've already felt it, haven't you? Those moments when you just know someone is lying. Or when you can feel the pain of a stranger without them saying a word."

Peter thought for a moment. There were indeed such moments, but he had always dismissed them as coincidences. "But why me? Why now?"

Helene looked at him lovingly. "Because the world needs people who listen and understand. You will decide how to use this gift. But you must accept it in order to understand it."

Peter wanted to say something, but Helene raised her hand. "I don't have much time left. But there is one thing you must know: The truth can be hard, Peter. But to know it and use it wisely is the greatest gift you can give someone."

Her image began to fade, as if an invisible wind had swept her away. "Wait!" Peter cried. "I still have so many questions!"

"You will find the answers, my boy," whispered her voice, now coming from afar. "Listen to your heart. And trust yourself."

When she was gone, Peter was left alone. But something had changed. He looked at the family portrait, and for the first time, he recognized his grandmother's smile as an invitation: Find your way.

The gift lay dormant within him, and Peter knew that from that moment on, his life would never be the same.

At the End of the Tunnel

Joseph loved his daily walks through the city. He had made it a habit to clear his head and let his thoughts wander. It was a mild autumn evening, the leaves rustling under his steps, and the streetlights cast a gentle glow on the sidewalk. Then, it happened.

A sudden pain shot through his chest. He stopped, his hand seeking support on a lamp post, but the world began to spin. Everything turned black.

When he opened his eyes, he was no longer in the city. Before him stretched a long, radiant tunnel, at the end of which shone a warm, inviting light. Joseph felt no fear, but a deep calm, unlike anything he had ever felt before.

In the light, he vaguely recognized figures that seemed familiar. As he stepped closer, he saw them clearly: his grandfather Karl with his cap, his grandmother Lotte with her unmistakable smile, and even his uncle

Heinrich, who had always told stories from long ago.

"Joseph," said Karl, his voice sounding like a distant echo. "You're here far too early."

"What... what do you mean?" Joseph stammered.

Lotte stepped forward and placed her hand on his shoulder. "Your time has not yet come, my boy. You still have so much ahead of you."

Joseph was confused. "But... I'm here, with you. Why should I go back?"

Heinrich laughed softly. "Because you are needed out there. Life is a gift, Joseph. A gift that shouldn't be thrown away carelessly."

Before Joseph could respond, he felt an invisible force pulling him back, away from the light, away from his ancestors. Their faces faded, but he still heard his grandfather's voice: "Use your time, Joseph. Live it wisely."

With a jolt, Joseph was back in reality. His eyes opened, and the first thing he saw were unfamiliar faces bending over him.

"He's breathing again!" a woman exclaimed in relief.

Joseph felt someone holding his hand. A man, probably one of the passersby, looked at him compassionately. "You had a heart failure. We resuscitated you. You're back."

Back. The word echoed in Joseph's head. He remembered the tunnel, the light, the faces of his ancestors. They had sent him back.

"Thank you," he murmured weakly, though he wasn't sure if he was thanking the passerby or his ancestors.

In the days and weeks that followed, Joseph began to reconsider his life thoroughly. He quit his stressful job that had always pulled him further away from himself. He reconnected with old friends, made peace with people he had been in conflict with, and began to live more consciously in the moment.

He didn't tell anyone about his experience, but in quiet moments, he often looked up at the sky and whispered, "Thank you for sending me back."

The memory of his ancestors remained alive within him, and every time he placed his hand on his chest, he felt not only his own heartbeat, but also the quiet reminder: Live your life as if it were the greatest gift.

The Great-Grandmother

It was a quiet Sunday morning, and the family was gathered around the breakfast table. The sun shone through the curtains, and the scent of fresh rolls and coffee filled the kitchen. Gesine, the five-year-old daughter of the family, sat at her place, pushing a jam sandwich around on her plate. Her blonde curls fell into her face as she chewed thoughtfully.

Suddenly, she put the sandwich down, looked up, and said with a childlike nonchalance, "I talked to Great-Grandmother last night."

The conversations stopped, and everyone at the table looked at her in surprise.

"With Great-Grandmother?" asked her mother, Hannah, almost spilling her coffee. "You mean my grandmother?"

Gesine nodded eagerly. "Yes, the woman in the picture in the living room. She visited me when I was asleep."

Hannah was speechless. The photo of her grandmother Marta did indeed hang in the living room, but Gesine had never shown much interest in it. And they hadn't talked about Marta in a long time.

"And what did she say?" asked Gesine's father, Daniel, with a crooked smile, as if trying to lighten the tension.

Gesine leaned forward and whispered as if it were a secret, "She said I don't have to be afraid of the dark. And that she used to always have a little light in the window when she was scared."

Hannah dropped her fork. "That... that can't be," she murmured, looking at Daniel with wide eyes.

"Why not?" Daniel asked, unsure whether to take the whole thing seriously.

Hannah swallowed. "The light... my grandmother told me that when I was a child. If she was afraid at night, she would put a little oil lamp in the window. But I never told Gesine about that."

"She also said she always drank chamomile tea when she had a stomach ache," Gesine added, taking a bite of her bread.

Hannah put a hand to her mouth. Her grandmother had comforted her the same way when she was a child—with chamomile tea.

"Gesine," Hannah said after a moment, her voice trembling slightly. "Did she tell you anything else?"

The little girl nodded and smiled. "She said she loves me, even though she's never seen me. And that she always looks after me."

Hannah felt tears well up in her eyes. She took Gesine in her arms and held her tightly.

Daniel cleared his throat and looked at the photo in the living room. "Maybe... maybe there are things we can't explain," he said quietly after a while.

The rest of the day seemed to be filled with a special stillness. In the evening, when Gesine was put to bed, she asked for a little lamp next to her window.

"So Great-Grandmother knows that I love her too," she explained.

Hannah placed the lamp, and as Gesine fell asleep, she gazed out the window and whispered, "Thank you for finding us."

In the distance, a small star seemed to shine brighter than the others.

A Laugh from the Past

A few weeks had passed since Gesine first talked about her encounter with her great-grandmother. The family had discussed the experience repeatedly, but no one knew what to make of it. Was it just a child's vivid imagination? Or had Gesine truly experienced something extraordinary?

One evening, after Gesine had fallen peacefully asleep, it happened again.

The next morning, she came cheerfully into the kitchen, her blonde curls tousled, clutching her rag doll tightly. "Mom, Dad!" she called. "Great-grandma came back!"

Hannah and Daniel exchanged glances. "Did she tell you something again?" Hannah asked cautiously while setting the table.

Gesine nodded excitedly and climbed onto her chair. "Yes! She told me a really funny story about great-grandpa."

"About great-grandpa?" Daniel frowned. "What kind of story?"

Gesine grinned widely. "She said he once tried to bring a cow into the kitchen because he thought it was hungry!"

Hannah froze mid-movement, the coffee pot in her hand. "What did you just say?"

"He wanted to bring a cow into the kitchen," Gesine repeated happily. "But the cow didn't want to come in, and then he got so mad that the neighbors all started laughing."

Hannah lowered the pot and slowly sat down on a chair. Her hands trembled slightly. "That... that actually happened," she said softly. "My grandmother told me this story when I was a teenager. Your great-grandfather, Marta's husband, really did try to bring a cow into the house because he thought it was hungry. Nobody except me and my mother knew about it."

Daniel looked at Hannah in astonishment. "This can't be real. Gesine, how do you know that?"

Gesine shrugged. "Great-grandma told me. She laughed so hard when she said it that I had to laugh too!"

Hannah stared at her daughter for a long time. In that moment, she realized that Gesine was special. She had a connection to her great-grandmother that no one could explain.

"Gesine," Hannah finally said, her voice soft. "Did you know that your great-grandmother was a little like you? She sometimes knew things she couldn't possibly have known. And she always said it was a gift."

"A gift?" Gesine tilted her head.

"Yes, a gift," Hannah said. "But a very special one. It means that you have a connection to the people who came before us. And sometimes, they tell us things to help us or to make us laugh."

Gesine smiled. "Then I'm happy to have the gift. Great-grandma says laughter is important."

Hannah leaned forward and hugged her daughter tightly. "Yes, my dear. It truly is. And you will learn to use this gift well."

From that day on, Gesine's special ability was no longer seen as strange but as wonderful by the family. The stories she shared from her great-grandmother not only brought laughter but also comfort into their lives. And every time Gesine spoke of a new encounter, it felt as if the family grew closer—as if the past and present were intertwined through the little girl with the big gift.

A Memory of Brest

Hans loved discovering new places. When he arrived in Brest with his wife Marie, he was immediately captivated by the rugged beauty of the Breton coast. The towering cliffs, the ancient fortifications, and the salty sea air felt strangely familiar to him.

But it wasn't just a feeling of déjà vu—it was something more.

On the third day of their stay, they decided to explore the old town. While Marie enthusiastically browsed for souvenirs in a small shop, Hans stopped in front of the Church of Saint-Sauveur. The ancient facade, with its weathered stones and bell tower, held a magnetic pull over him.

"I know this place," he murmured to himself.

"Of course," said an older man beside him, smiling kindly. "This church is one of the oldest buildings in Brest."

Hans nodded absentmindedly. But it wasn't the information that preoccupied him—it was a memory, flooding over him like a storm breaking out of nowhere.

He saw himself—or rather, a man who looked like him but wasn't quite the same. The man wore a rough linen shirt, a cloak, and carried a heavy bag. His hair was longer, and his hands were roughened by hard labor. Hans heard the sound of hammers, saw ships being built in a harbor, and felt the salty wind against his skin.

"Jacques," he suddenly whispered.

"What did you say?" Marie asked, emerging from the shop and looking at him curiously. "Jacques," Hans repeated, his voice trembling. "That was my name."

"Which name?" Marie placed a hand on his arm, but Hans seemed entranced.

"I was here," he said softly. "A long time ago. I lived here. I was a shipbuilder. My name was Jacques."

Marie stared at him, unsure if he was joking. But Hans looked completely serious.

They spent the rest of the day walking through the old town, with Hans recounting things he couldn't possibly have known.

"This used to be a marketplace," he said, pointing to an open square. "Merchants sold their goods here. And over there," he gestured toward a narrow alley, "was the blacksmith's shop. I often went there to get nails for the ships."

"How do you know this?" Marie finally asked, both fascinated and unsettled.

Hans paused. "I don't know. It's as if these memories have suddenly returned. Like a veil has been lifted."

That evening, they dined at a small restaurant near the harbor. Hans gazed out at the water, which glittered in the light of the setting sun. "I remember my death," he said quietly.

Marie froze. "What do you mean by that?"

"I…" Hans swallowed. "I was on a ship. There was a storm. We were trying to secure the sails, but a wave caught me and swept me into the sea. I drowned."

Marie took his hand. "That's… incredible. But Hans, what does it mean?"

Hans looked at her with serious eyes. "I'm not entirely sure. But I think I was meant to return here. Maybe to understand something. Or to make peace with that past."

In the days that followed, they explored Brest and its history together. Hans felt strangely fulfilled, as though he had reclaimed a part of himself that he'd lost.

As they finally left the city, Hans cast one last look at the place that had given him so much more than he had expected.
"Do I really only live once?" he asked himself softly. But in his heart, he already knew the answer.

The Voice at the Cabin

Yvonne loved skiing. The crisp mountain air, the snow-covered peaks, and the sound of the wind rushing past as she sped down the slopes were like balm for her soul. On this winter day, the sky was a brilliant blue, and the slopes in Austria were perfectly groomed. After several runs, she decided to take a break. She made her way to a rustic mountain cabin, its smoking chimney promising warmth and coziness. With an elegant turn, she stopped in front of the cabin, brushed the snow off her skis, and stepped inside.

The room was bustling with activity. The scent of Kaiserschmarrn and mulled wine filled the air, and the voices of skiers blended into a warm hum. Yvonne found an empty spot in the corner, where a small table stood slightly apart from the crowd.

She had barely sat down when she noticed an older woman at the neighboring table. The woman was wrapped in a long, dark coat and wore a headscarf that framed her silver hair. Her eyes were clear and piercing, and she seemed to be looking directly at Yvonne.

"You're Yvonne, aren't you?" the woman suddenly asked.

Yvonne was startled. "Yes, that's me. Do we know each other?"

The woman smiled mysteriously. "Not directly. But I know your grandmother."

Yvonne frowned. "My grandmother? She passed away years ago."

The woman nodded. "I know. But she wanted me to tell you something."

Yvonne caught her breath. "What… what do you mean?"

"Your grandmother and I are connected, let's put it that way," the woman replied. "She has a message for you. Something you need to know."

Yvonne was skeptical, but something in the woman's voice kept her from getting up and leaving. "What do I need to know?" she finally asked.

The woman leaned in slightly. "Your grandmother always had a bracelet that meant a lot to her. It's silver, with a small star-shaped charm. She lost it years ago and never spoke of it because she thought it was gone forever. But she wants you to find it."

Yvonne shook her head. "A bracelet? I've never heard of it. And how am I supposed to find it?"

The woman smiled. "It's in a small wooden box in the old dresser on your attic. Your grandmother put it there and forgot about it. If you find it, it will remind you of her—and of her love for you."

Yvonne stared at the woman, speechless. "That… that could be true," she murmured. "We have that old dresser, but I've never looked through the drawers."

The woman stood up, pulled her coat tighter around herself, and nodded at Yvonne. "Sometimes the connections between generations are stronger than we think. Go home and look for it. You'll be surprised."

Before Yvonne could say anything, the woman turned and left the cabin.

Yvonne sat there for a while, unable to process what had just happened. Eventually, she took the last run down to the valley, but the woman's words stayed with her.

When she got home, she climbed up to the attic and found the old dresser that she hadn't touched in years. Her hands trembled as she searched through the drawers. And there, in the very back of the bottom drawer, was a small wooden box.

When she opened it, she found a silver bracelet with a star-shaped charm—just as the woman had described.

Tears welled up in Yvonne's eyes. She held the bracelet tightly and felt a profound connection to her grandmother, as if she were still there.

From that day on, Yvonne wore the bracelet, not just as a reminder of her grandmother but also of the encounter at the mountain cabin —a sign that her grandmother's love had never truly disappeared.

Final Farewell in Vienna

Dorit was excited. The class trip to Vienna was a highlight of the year. The magnificent buildings, the famous art, and the vibrant atmosphere of the city fascinated her. But beneath the cheerful surface, there was a shadow that accompanied her and her class: Anna, her classmate and friend, had passed away just weeks before the trip. After a long battle with an illness, she had not made it.

Anna had been so looking forward to this trip. She had often talked with Dorit about which sights they absolutely wanted to see— the Hofburg, St. Stephen's Cathedral, and the Schönbrunn Palace. Now, she wasn't there, and her absence was palpable to the whole class.

On the third evening in Vienna, the students had some free time. Dorit decided to wander alone through the narrow alleys of the old town. She wanted to leave the hustle and bustle of the group behind for a moment.

She eventually found herself in a small square where an old street lamp cast a soft light on the cobbled paths. It was quiet, only the faint hum of the city and the distant ringing of a church bell could be heard. Dorit sat on a bench and let her thoughts wander.

"It's beautiful here, isn't it?"

The voice made her jump. She turned around —and froze.

There stood Anna. She was wearing her favorite coat, the one she always wore when it was cool, and a gentle smile was on her face. She looked pale, almost translucent, but her eyes still sparkled, just like before.

"A-Anna?" Dorit could barely utter a word.

"Yes, it's me," Anna said calmly. "Don't be afraid, Dorit. I just wanted to stop by for a moment."

Dorit felt her heart race. "But... how? You're...?"

"...not here anymore," Anna finished the sentence. "I know. But I wanted to say goodbye. I couldn't do that before I left. And I wanted to thank you."

"Thank me? For what?"

Anna sat next to Dorit, but Dorit felt no pressure on the bench. It was as if Anna was made of light and air.

"For your friendship," Anna said. "You were always there for me, even in the tough times. And you made me laugh when I thought I could never laugh again."

Dorit felt tears welling up in her eyes. "Anna, I'm so sorry. I wish you were here with us. We could have seen so much together."

Anna smiled gently. "I am here, Dorit. Just in a different way. I experienced the trip through you. You saw everything I wanted to see. And I was with you."

The Voice of the Sea

Warnemünde was bathed in soft light on this spring day. The sun shimmered on the waves of the Baltic Sea, seagulls circled over the harbor, and a fresh breeze blew over the Mittel Mole. Hubert stood by the railing, his gaze fixed on the endless expanse of the sea.

He often came here, to this place that held so much meaning for him. Here, a few years ago, he had said goodbye to his wife, Anne. It had been her wish: a sea burial, free and in harmony with the nature she had loved so much.

"Anne," Hubert whispered, his voice almost swallowed by the wind. "I wish you could be here. I miss you."

He closed his eyes and listened to the waves gently hitting the stones. Suddenly, he felt something—an inexplicable tingling in the air that flowed through him as if an invisible hand were touching him.

"I'm here, Hubert."

Hubert's eyes flew open. The voice was clear, gentle, and familiar. His heart skipped a beat, and he turned around—but there was no one.

"Anne?" he asked, unsure if he was dreaming or awake.

"Yes, my dear. It's really me," the voice answered. It seemed to come from everywhere, yet directly from his heart.

"How... how is this possible?" Hubert whispered, tears welling in his eyes.

"Sometimes a window opens between our worlds," Anne explained. "And today... today I felt that you needed me."

Hubert leaned against the railing, his gaze still fixed on the water. "I don't know how to go on without you. It feels so empty, Anne."

"Oh, Hubert," she said lovingly. "You're never without me. I'm always with you. In your heart, in your memories... and in moments like this."

Hubert swallowed hard. "I should have told you so much more when you were still here. How much I love you. How thankful I am for you."

"I know, Hubert," Anne said. "I've always known. Your love was in every glance, every word, every gesture. You don't need to blame yourself."

They stood like that for a while—Hubert on the Mittel Mole, surrounded by the voice of his deceased wife. Time seemed to stand still.

"Why are you here today?" he finally asked.

"To remind you that you must go on living," she answered. "I want you to be happy. Go out, experience the world, find peace. You have so much love inside you, Hubert. It would be a shame not to share it."

"I don't know if I can," Hubert admitted.

"Yes, you can," Anne said gently, but with emphasis. "You have a strength inside you that you haven't yet realized. And whenever you doubt, think of me. I will always guide you, just like the wind guides the waves."

Hubert closed his eyes and took a deep breath. The salty air filled his lungs, and a sense of calm flowed through him.

"I will try," he said quietly.

"That's all I wish for," Anne said. "And don't forget, Hubert: The love we share doesn't end with death. It is eternal."

A gentle gust of wind brushed across his face, as if Anne had touched him one last time. Hubert opened his eyes, and the sea shimmered under the sun, as though it were making him a silent promise.

He stood there on the Mittel Mole for a long time, but in his heart, he no longer felt alone. Anne was with him—and always would be.

The Camino de Santiago

Karin was on the Camino de Santiago, just like so many before her. It was a journey she had undertaken out of an inner longing—a search for answers, for peace, perhaps even for herself. The ancient paths of Spain, lined with olive trees and wind-swept fields, seemed full of stories waiting to be heard if she only listened closely enough.

On this day, the path led her through a dense oak forest. The sun cast dancing shadows on the trail, and the soft rustling of leaves was her only companion. She had the feeling that this part of the journey was different— quieter, almost reverential.

Suddenly, Karin felt the air around her grow cooler. The wind carried with it a strange melody, a hum that almost sounded like voices. She stopped, closed her eyes, and listened.

"Karin," whispered a voice.

Startled, she opened her eyes and looked around. But she was alone.

"Karin," came the voice again, this time clearer. It was a deep, calm voice, followed by another, higher one. "Listen to us."

"Who... who is there?" she asked hesitantly.

"We are your ancestors," answered the first voice. "We walked this path before you, long ago."

Karin was speechless. She had often heard of spiritual experiences on the Camino, but this felt different.

"Are your voices... just my thoughts?" she asked quietly.

"No, child," said the second voice, now warmer, like that of an older woman. "We are here to tell you something. Something you need to know."

"What do you want to tell me?" Karin whispered, her hands trembling slightly.

"Hundreds of years ago, we pilgrimaged the same path," began the first voice. "Your great-great-grandfather, Miguel, carried a stone from his homeland in his hands—a symbol of the burden he carried. He laid it down at the Cruz de Ferro and found peace."

"And I," said the second voice, "was Magdalena, one of your ancient foremothers. I walked this path when I was young and full of doubt. In Santiago, I found the strength to begin a new life."

Karin couldn't hold back her tears. The words touched something deep inside her, something she could hardly describe.

"Why are you telling me this?" she finally asked.

"Because you too carry a burden," Magdalena said. "A burden that prevents you from being truly free."

"But I don't know how to let it go," Karin admitted.

"The way will show you," Miguel said. "We are here to remind you that you are not alone. The strength of our journey lives on in you. Every step you take carries us—and our love for you."

Karin felt a wave of warmth wash over her. She closed her eyes and let the tears flow freely. When she opened her eyes again, the light filtering through the trees seemed brighter, and the voices had fallen silent.

But she no longer felt alone. Her steps had new energy, and her heart was lighter as she continued on her way.

Days later, when she arrived at the Cruz de Ferro, she took a small stone from her backpack. With trembling hands, she placed it on the pile and whispered, "For you. And for me."

In that moment, she felt connected to her ancestors, to the path, and to herself. It was as if the voices of the Camino had revealed an ancient secret: that the path was not just a trail through the landscape, but also a journey to the heart—back to the roots and forward into the future.

The Message at the Etsch

Gernot was leisurely riding his bike along the path from Merano to Bolzano. The air was clear and warm, the Adige sparkled in the sunlight, and the mountains cast their shadows over the river. It felt like a day when the world was light and peaceful.

But shortly after a small rest area, he noticed a figure by the side of the path. An older man sat on a large stone, his weathered face partly hidden beneath a straw hat, with a worn backpack at his feet. He looked exhausted.

Gernot stopped. "Is everything all right?" he asked kindly.

The old man raised his head. His eyes, clear yet full of strange depth, met Gernot's gaze. It felt as though they could see right through him. "A little tired, young man," he said in a rough voice. "But I need to wait here. I knew you would come."

Gernot frowned. "Me? How do you know who I am?"

The man smiled faintly. "Sometimes one is given a task they don't fully understand. But I have something to tell you—something that belongs to you."

Skeptical yet curious, Gernot got off his bike and sat on a nearby stone. "What do you want to tell me?"

The old man took a sip of water from a small bottle and began. "Your grandfather Viktor, correct? He died in the war. In Russia."

Gernot felt his heart race. "That's true. But I hardly know anything about it. He died before my father was even born."

The man nodded thoughtfully. "It was a bitterly cold winter. Viktor was part of a retreat where many men lost their lives. But your grandfather did something that set him apart. He sacrificed his life to save others."

Gernot was speechless. "How… how do you know this? No one in my family knows the details."

The wanderer sighed. "I'm just a messenger. Sometimes the afterlife speaks to us— through dreams, visions, or people like me. In a quiet moment, I received the task of telling you this story."

He went on to describe how Viktor, during the retreat, saved a group of comrades from a hopeless situation. He drew the enemy's attention to himself, fully aware he would not return. But his sacrifice saved many lives.

"His comrades never forgot him," the old man added. "And this message I bring to you is a kind of thanks. His courage, his kindness —they must not be lost. You need to know that he was a hero."

Gernot felt a storm of emotions rising within him: pride, sadness, reverence. "But why now? Why here?"

The wanderer rested his hands on his stick and looked at Gernot intently. "Perhaps because you need to hear it now. Perhaps to remind you that you carry a legacy—not just his blood, but also his strength and courage. The afterlife has its ways of reaching us. Now it's up to you to carry this story forward."

Before Gernot could ask another question, the old man stood up. His movements were suddenly smooth, almost effortless. His eyes seemed to glow with an unearthly light.

"I must go," he said calmly. "But don't forget what you've learned today. Your grandfather lives on in you, and now you know why."

With those words, the man turned and walked along the path until he disappeared around a bend.

Gernot remained seated, overwhelmed by the encounter. The man's words echoed in his mind. When he finally got back on his bike and continued his ride, he felt different—as though he had regained not just a story, but a part of his grandfather.

The Adige sparkled brighter than before, as if it wanted to whisper something to him. And Gernot knew he would never forget the messenger's words.

The Waves of the Past

Heinz was visiting Gruissan for the first time, a small fishing village on the southern French Mediterranean coast. The narrow streets with their pastel-colored houses, the gentle lapping of boats in the harbor, and the salty scent of the sea air had immediately enchanted him. He was merely passing through, but something had drawn him here—a feeling he couldn't quite explain.

One afternoon, he was strolling along the harbor when he noticed an older fisherman hauling in his nets. The man's face, weathered by sun and wind, radiated a calm that fascinated Heinz.

"Beautiful day, isn't it?" the fisherman called out in French when he noticed Heinz.

"Yes, wonderful," Heinz replied, his school-level French still passable.

The fisherman waved him closer. "You're not from around here, that much is clear. What brings you to Gruissan?"

"Just curiosity," Heinz said with a smile. "I'm traveling around and heard that Gruissan is beautiful."

The fisherman nodded, observed Heinz silently for a moment, and then said, "You know, sometimes curiosity leads us to places that have more to do with us than we realize."

Heinz frowned. "What do you mean?"

The fisherman pulled a small fish from the net, tossed it back into the water, and said, "When I saw you, I immediately thought of a man my grandfather used to tell stories about. A man named Étienne. He lived here in Gruissan a very, very long time ago."

"Étienne?" Heinz shook his head. "The name doesn't mean anything to me."

"But your face—it's like seeing him again," the fisherman said, gesturing to a bench nearby. "Sit down, and I'll tell you about him."

Curious and slightly bewildered, Heinz sat down. The fisherman began his story: "Étienne was a fisherman, like me. But he had something that set him apart. He could read the sea like a book. He always knew when a storm was coming, where the best fishing grounds were, and what dangers lay ahead. People said he had a special connection to the sea—almost as if it spoke to him."

Heinz listened intently.

"One day," the fisherman continued, "Étienne was caught far out at sea. A storm came up suddenly, and he was alone in his small boat. People thought he was lost. But days later, they found him—alive, but changed. He spoke of how the sea had shown him something—a truth about his family, about his future. He swore that one day, one of his descendants would return to continue that connection."

The fisherman looked at Heinz with a mysterious smile. "And now, here you are." Heinz felt a shiver run down his spine. "That's… incredible," he stammered. "But how can you be sure I'm his descendant?" The fisherman shrugged. "The sea knows the answers. I'm just a man who casts nets and keeps stories alive. But sometimes it brings people back to places they can't explain. Maybe you're here to renew that connection."

Heinz felt as though the world had momentarily paused. The fisherman's words echoed within him.

"What should I do?" he asked at last.

"Go to the beach at sunset," the fisherman said. "Sit down and listen to the waves. Perhaps the sea will tell you what it showed Étienne."

That evening, Heinz followed the fisherman's advice. On the beach, under a sky ablaze with red and gold, he sat in the sand and let the sound of the waves wash over him.

And in the silence, in the connection between sea and sky, he thought he heard a voice—a whisper that told him a story he didn't yet fully understand but that felt strangely familiar.

It was as if the sea were whispering to him: "Welcome back."

The next morning, Heinz returned to the harbor, determined to learn more about his mysterious ancestor Étienne and his connection to Gruissan. The fisherman, who introduced himself as Jules, was already mending his nets when Heinz greeted him.

"I'm back," Heinz said with a smile. "I could hardly sleep last night. I need to know more about Étienne."

Jules nodded, as though he had expected this.

"Sit down," he said, patting a wooden crate beside him, and pulled a small wooden box from his boat. "I have something that might help you."

From the box, he retrieved an old, yellowed parchment. It was a sea chart, showing the coastline around Gruissan, but it also bore small markings that made no sense to Heinz. "What's this?" Heinz asked, carefully unfolding the chart.
"Étienne made this map," Jules explained. "It shows not only the sea and fishing grounds but also his memories—places that were significant to him."

Jules pointed to a marking inland. "Here," he said, "is the house where he lived. It's long since fallen into ruin, but the stones still hold his story."
Heinz was overwhelmed. "Can we go there?"
"Of course," Jules said. "I'll take you."

That afternoon, Jules and Heinz set out. The path led through a rugged, stony landscape, past fragrant lavender and olive groves stretching beneath the hot sun. After about an hour, they reached a hilltop, where a dilapidated stone house came into view.

"That's it," Jules said. "This is where Étienne lived."

Heinz approached the house slowly, feeling a strange mix of awe and connection. He touched the cool stones, covered in moss, and imagined his ancestor's life there. "Étienne wasn't just a fisherman," Jules said quietly. "He was also a man who preserved people's stories. He wrote letters, recorded memories. Maybe you'll find more here."

In one corner of the house, where the roof was still partially intact, Heinz discovered a small chest hidden under an old beam. It was rusty, but with some effort, he opened it. Inside were yellowed papers, written in elegant handwriting.
"This is Étienne's writing," Jules said, his eyes bright with excitement.

Heinz began to read. The texts were personal notes from Étienne, describing not only his life as a fisherman but also his family.
"I have roots in Germany," Heinz read aloud. "My great-grandfather emigrated here from a small village on the Danube. I carry the memories of my ancestors within me, but my heart now belongs to this sea."

Heinz paused. He had never known that his family had once migrated from Germany to France.

"That's you," Jules said with a knowing smile. "You're the connection between these worlds. Your roots are here and there, and Étienne knew that one day someone would return to rediscover this bond."

Back in Gruissan, Heinz felt changed. He had not only learned a fascinating story about his great-great-great-grandfather but had also uncovered a deeper truth about himself. His roots were more complex and richer than he had ever imagined.

That evening, as the sun set over the harbor, Heinz stood by the water, feeling a strange sense of peace. He thought of Étienne, his love for the sea, and the bridge he had built between cultures.

"Thank you," Heinz whispered into the sound of the waves. It was as if the sea answered him, softly but surely, like an echo from the past: "Welcome home."

The Whisper in the Minster

Leo was a curious young man of 28, traveling through Mecklenburg-Vorpommern in search of his family roots. His research had brought him to Bad Doberan, where someone had mentioned that his ancestors might have originated from the region.

One afternoon, he entered the famous Minster of Bad Doberan, drawn by the peace and beauty of the Gothic building. The towering columns and colorful windows seemed to tell stories from another time. Leo sat down on a bench, letting his gaze wander and enjoying the silence, interrupted only occasionally by the soft steps of other visitors.

Suddenly, he noticed a figure standing in front of one of the altars. It was an older man in a simple gray coat. His face appeared dignified, yet strangely familiar. The man turned around, and his eyes seemed to look directly at Leo.

"Are you seeking answers?" the figure asked, his voice gentle and deep.

Leo was taken aback. "Excuse me, do we know each other?"

The man smiled. "Not directly, but I know you, Leo. You are a part of me—just as I am a part of you."

Confused, Leo stood and approached the man. "What do you mean by that?"

"I am Heinrich," the man said. "Many, many years ago, I lived in this region. You carry my blood in your veins. I am your great-great-great-grandfather."

Leo felt a lump form in his throat. The man's—or rather, the soul's—words were soothing, but they were so incredible that Leo's mind refused to accept them.

"I'm not sure I can believe that," Leo finally said, his voice hesitant. "How can I be certain that you're really... my ancestor? This could all just be my imagination."

Heinrich nodded understandingly, as if he had expected this reaction. "That's a valid question, Leo. You are a smart man, and smart people doubt. But I can give you proof—something only you can find."

"What kind of proof?" Leo asked skeptically.

Heinrich smiled faintly. "In the crypt of the Minster, on the eastern wall, there is a stone that is slightly different from the others. If you search for it, you will find an inscription I left behind before I departed this world. It contains something only a member of my family would understand."

"An inscription?" Leo asked. "And what does it say?"

"You will have to see for yourself," Heinrich replied. "I won't spoil it for you. But I promise you won't be disappointed."

Leo frowned, unsure whether to trust the man. Yet something about Heinrich's calm, assured demeanor made him consider at least looking.

"Fine," Leo said at last. "I'll look. But if I find nothing…"

"…then you may doubt everything," Heinrich finished the sentence for him. "But I know you'll find it."

With those words, Heinrich's figure began to fade again, this time more slowly. "Good luck, Leo. And remember—answers are always closer than they seem."

With his heart pounding, Leo made his way to the crypt. It was a dim, silent room, filled with an air of history and time. The eastern wall was lined with smooth stones arranged in precise rows.

Leo began examining the wall, searching for any sign of a difference, as Heinrich had described. At first, nothing seemed unusual, but after a few minutes, he noticed a stone that was slightly lighter and smoother than the others.

His fingers cautiously traced the surface until he felt an engraved inscription. Narrowing his eyes, he read the words carved in archaic German:

"Vollmer – The blood unites us, and truth shines in the heart."

Leo froze. The name "Vollmer"—his family name—was unmistakable. And the meaning of the words was clear. It was a message meant just for him, an echo from the past now connecting to his present.

His heart raced. There was no way anyone could have placed this here for him intentionally. The engraving was old, the stone weathered—and yet the message was undeniable.

As Leo left the crypt, he felt transformed. The doubts that had plagued him earlier had vanished, replaced by a deep, inexplicable certainty. Heinrich had spoken the truth.

Standing in the daylight before the Minster, Leo paused and looked up at the sky. "Thank you, Heinrich," he whispered.

And for a moment, just briefly, he felt a gentle breeze brush his face, as if it were a quiet greeting from another world.

Afterword

Dear readers,

The stories in this collection arose from a deep curiosity about life's great questions: What happens to us when we leave this world? Where does the soul go – or does it even exist? These thoughts have accompanied me for a long time and were repeatedly reignited through numerous conversations with friends and moments of quiet reflection.

Each of these stories invites you to look beyond the familiar horizon and let yourself be carried by imagination and emotion. They are not answers but signposts – sometimes gentle, sometimes provocative – meant to inspire you to develop your own thoughts. For the true magic of literature lies in opening new perspectives and making us receptive to the unexpected.

It is my hope that this collection not only entertains you but also touches and enriches you. Perhaps one story made you smile or prompted you to pause and reflect. Perhaps it raised questions that linger within you for some time.

I sincerely thank you for embarking on this journey. And if you ever ponder your own answers to life's big questions, I hope these stories can be a small companion for you.

With my best wishes,
Norbert Kürlis